Marcy Finds Her Glow

Written by
Mallory Thayer

Illustrations by
Jeanine Henning

Marcy Finds Her Glow© Copyright 2024 Mallory Thayer

Copyright notice: All rights reserved under the International and Pan-American Copyright Conventions. No part of this book may be reproduced or transmitted in any form or by any means, electronic or mechanical, including photocopying and recording, or by any information storage and retrieval system, without permission in writing from the publisher.

This is a work of fiction. Names, places, characters, and incidents are either the product of the author's imagination or are used fictitiously, and any resemblance to any actual persons, living or dead, organizations, events, or locales is entirely coincidental.

Warning: the unauthorized reproduction or distribution of this copyrighted work is illegal. Criminal copyright infringement, including infringement without monetary gain, is investigated by the FBI and is punishable by up to 5 years in prison and a fine of $250,000.

ISBN: 979-8-89109-667-7 - paperback

ISBN: 979-8-89109-668-4 - ebook

ISBN: 979-8-89109-695-0 - hardcover

This book is dedicated to my mom, Janice, who always reminds me "I can only be who I am."

Create your own unique glow for Marcy!

You can bring the magic of Marcy to home, school - or wherever you bring your coloring supplies - with the Marcy and friends coloring pages!

Visit mallory-writes.com and enter your name and email address to receive your free download of 5 coloring pages that you can print and share.

mallory-writes.com

Marcy gazed wide-eyed at Roger and the other stars as they danced around the sky like fireflies on a summer night.

"Wow, look at how bright they shine!" Marcy muttered. She stood off to the side and hunched her shoulders, hoping no one would notice she was not glowing.

Up above, Roger flashed a smile and beamed so bright that he looked like a radiant ball of fire!

"One…two…three…GLLOOOWWW!" Roger called to the stargang.

"Come on, everyone, let the light flow! Let's put on a great show tonight!"

Roger spotted Marcy and flew in her direction. "Yo, Marcy, where's your glow?"

Roger grumbled, glaring at Marcy over his shades. "If you don't get glowing, you gotta get going. Only the brightest of stars can hang with this crew."

"Yeah, Marcy, show us what you got!" The stargang circled around Roger and Marcy.

"I can shine just as bright as you!" Marcy blurted, her eyes now dazzling with courage.

"Well, let's see it then," Roger snapped back. "On the count of three. One...two...three..."

Marcy tried with all her might, but she couldn't make a single ray of light. Instead, faint splotches of red, orange, blue, green, and every shade in between appeared all over her like a multicolor rash.

"Look at all those weird colors! She can't even glow right!" Roger and the stargang pointed and laughed as Marcy sank down and hung her head.

"Let's face it, Marcy." Roger shrugged, flipping his flowing locks. "You will never be bright and brilliant like us. You will only ever be dim, dull, and disappointing."

Marcy flew from the scene, finally letting the flood of tears stream down her face.

"I will NEVER fit in here," Marcy wailed, burying her face in a cloud. "I want to go as far away from this galaxy as I can and never come back!"

Marcy hopped up, wiped the tears from her face, and took off into the night.

Suddenly, she sensed something flying behind her. "Marcy, my dear," a soft yet booming voice said. "Where are you off to in such a hurry?"

Marcy recognized this calm voice and knew it was her longtime friend, Melvin the Meteor.

"Oh Melvin, it's just horrible," Marcy said, her lips quivering. "I don't belong here. I'm a star who can't even shine. Roger was right. I will only ever be dim, dull, and disappointing."

"Now Marcy, that's not true," Melvin reassured her. "Just because you are different, doesn't mean you don't belong."

"No, it is true," she cried, "I'm going to run away from this galaxy, and you can't stop me!"

Suddenly her eyes brightened with hope as an idea fluttered in her mind.

"Wait a second...Melvin, you're always flying somewhere new." A smirk formed on Marcy's face. "Maybe I could...hitch a ride?"

Without waiting for Melvin's response, she scrambled up Melvin's back, startling the mighty meteor.

"Marcy, get down!" Melvin scowled. "I don't think this is such a good idea!"

"Look over there, Melvin!" Marcy threw her arms up high as they sped along. "I can see the next galaxy!"

Distracted by Marcy, Melvin suddenly jerked to dodge an incoming comet. Marcy wobbled left and right, trying to keep her balance.

"I...I...Oh no—WAHHHH!!!"

Marcy tumbled like a baby bird from its nest, spinning and spiraling toward a shimmering blue surface below.

SPLASH!

Marcy smacked against the glassy surface. Eyes and fists clenched, she plunged through the water like a rocket crash landing on the moon.

Marcy finally hit the ground and a cloud of sand swirled around her. She opened her eyes slowly. "Where am I?"

Confused by the new atmosphere, Marcy moved her arms carefully from side to side. "This place feels a lot wetter than any galaxy I've ever been to."

Marcy looked left, looked right, then looked up at the glassy ceiling above. Suddenly, she realized where she was.

"Oh my gosh, am I on *Earth*?!" Marcy gasped. "I wanted to run away, but not to the ocean!"

Marcy trudged along the sandy floor of the sea, keeping her eyes peeled for anything—or anyone—that could help.

Finally, she saw a creature that looked like Melvin but with short green legs treading slowly in the water.

"Hello, Mr. Meteor?" Marcy spoke softly, raising her eyebrows. "Can you help me get back to my home in the sky?"

"I'm not a meteor, young lady. I'm a sea turtle." The turtle's words slid from his mouth slower than the setting sun. "I wish I could help you, dear, but my shell here is my home, and it's the only home I know."

"Well, that is nice for you!" Marcy planted her hands on her hips. "But that won't help me get out of this nightmare!"

Surprised by Marcy's snappy tone, the turtle raised his head and replied, "I'm sorry, miss, but I can only be who I am."

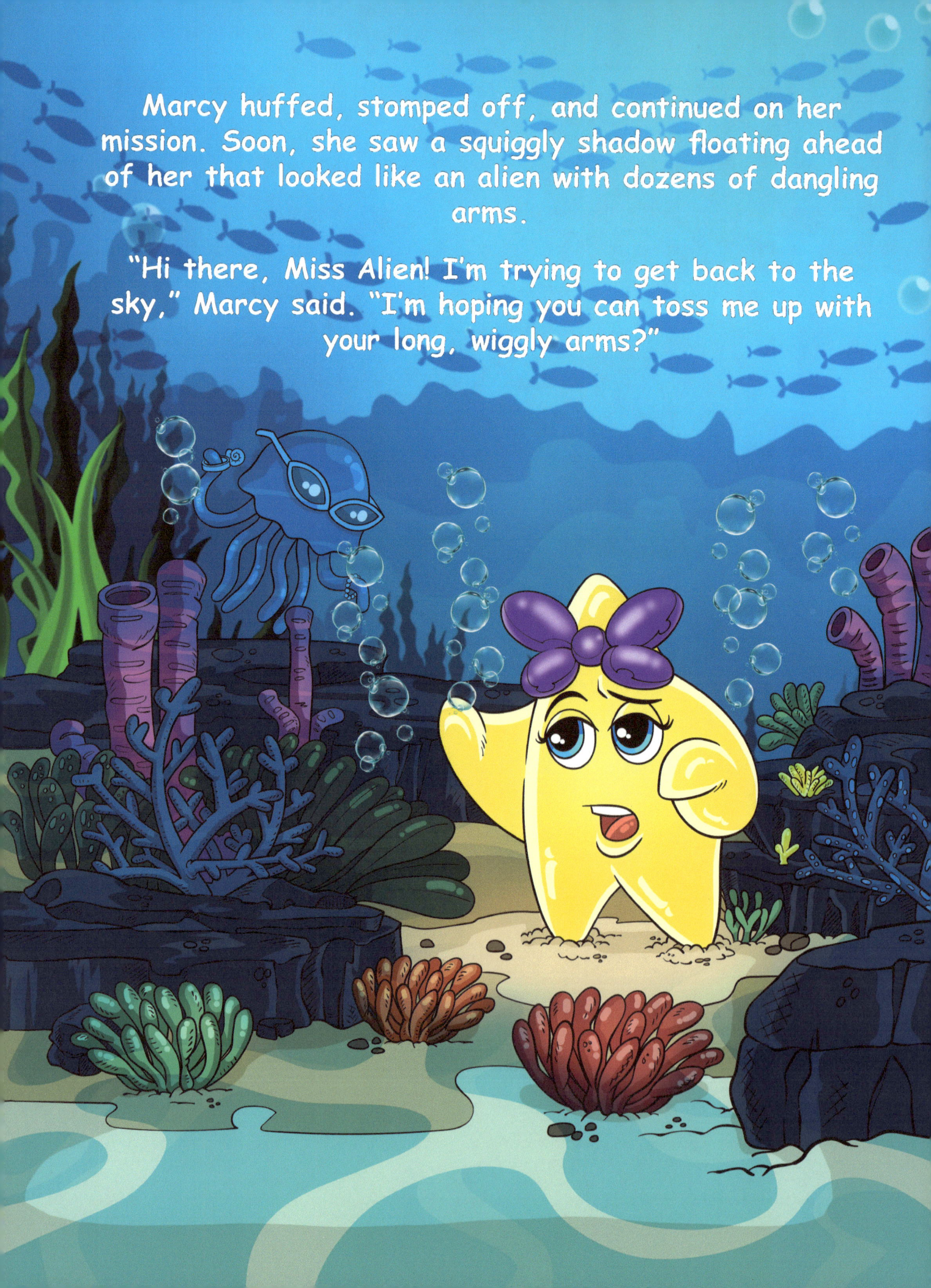

Marcy huffed, stomped off, and continued on her mission. Soon, she saw a squiggly shadow floating ahead of her that looked like an alien with dozens of dangling arms.

"Hi there, Miss Alien! I'm trying to get back to the sky," Marcy said. "I'm hoping you can toss me up with your long, wiggly arms?"

"Oh, sweetie," the jiggly jellyfish sighed. "I'm no alien, and these aren't arms at all. They are tentacles. If you touched my tentacles, they would certainly sting you!"

"Ugh!" Marcy scoffed. "Why can't anyone help me?!"

"I'm sorry, angel." The jellyfish shrugged. "But I can only be who I am."

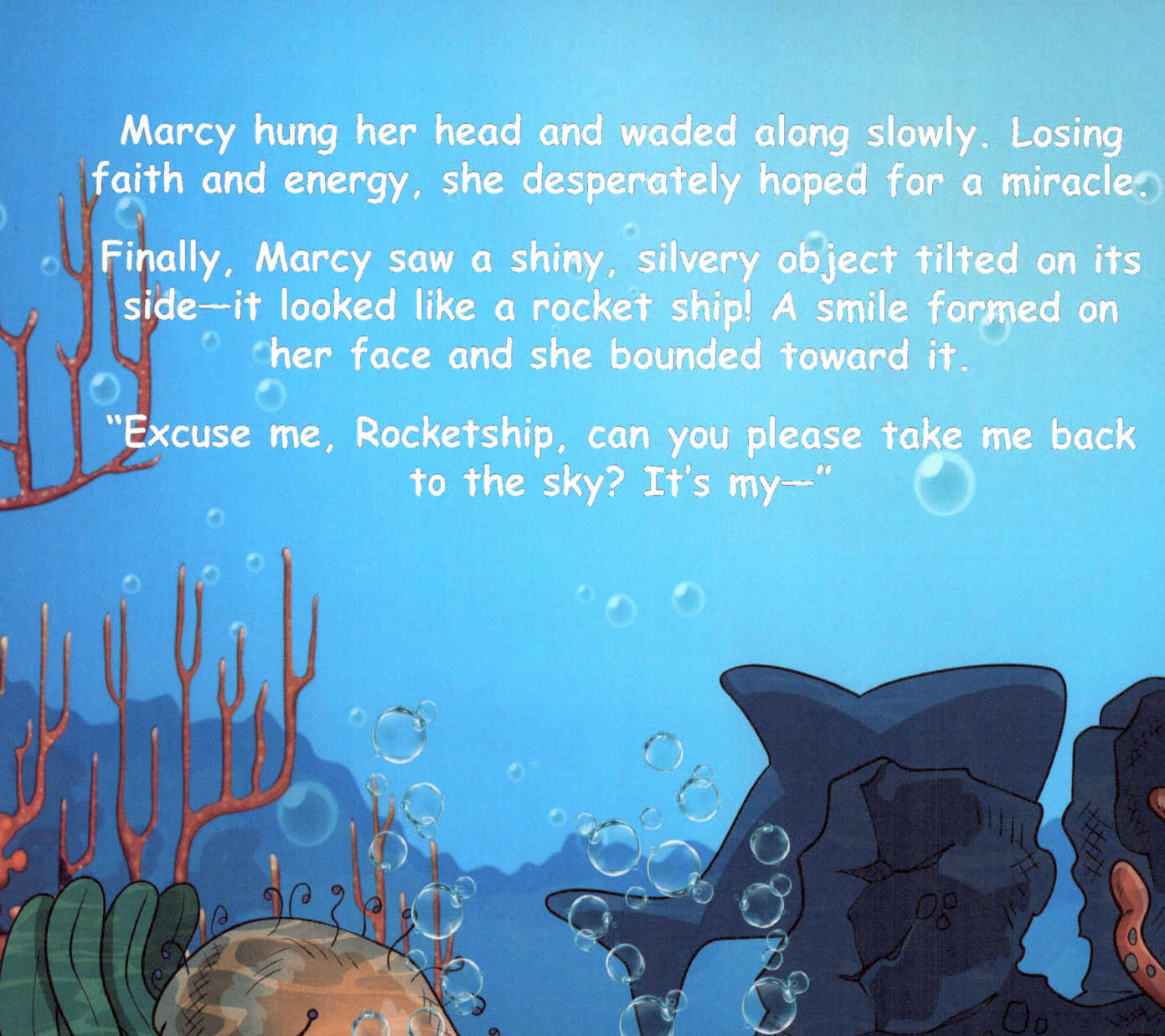

Marcy hung her head and waded along slowly. Losing faith and energy, she desperately hoped for a miracle.

Finally, Marcy saw a shiny, silvery object tilted on its side—it looked like a rocket ship! A smile formed on her face and she bounded toward it.

"Excuse me, Rocketship, can you please take me back to the sky? It's my—"

"Oh no, miss, I am just a silly shark! I didn't mean to scare you," the saddened shark stuttered through his sharp teeth. "I can only be who I am. Did you say you need help getting back to the sky?"

But Marcy darted away before she could hear him.

Marcy hid deep in a sea cave, and her thoughts became as dark as the shadows around her.

"I wish I had never left home!" she shouted to herself. "I don't care if I'm not as bright as the other stars, or if my glow is a splotchy mess. I don't care if I am dull and dim!" Marcy shut her eyes tight and scrunched her face. "I just want...to...go..."

"HOOOOMMMEEE!"

Marcy opened her eyes and was shocked by her own power and light.

"Oh my gosh, look at my glow!" Marcy jumped and chills ran up her arms. The most magnificent spectrum of colors radiated from her skin, brighter than any other star she had ever seen.

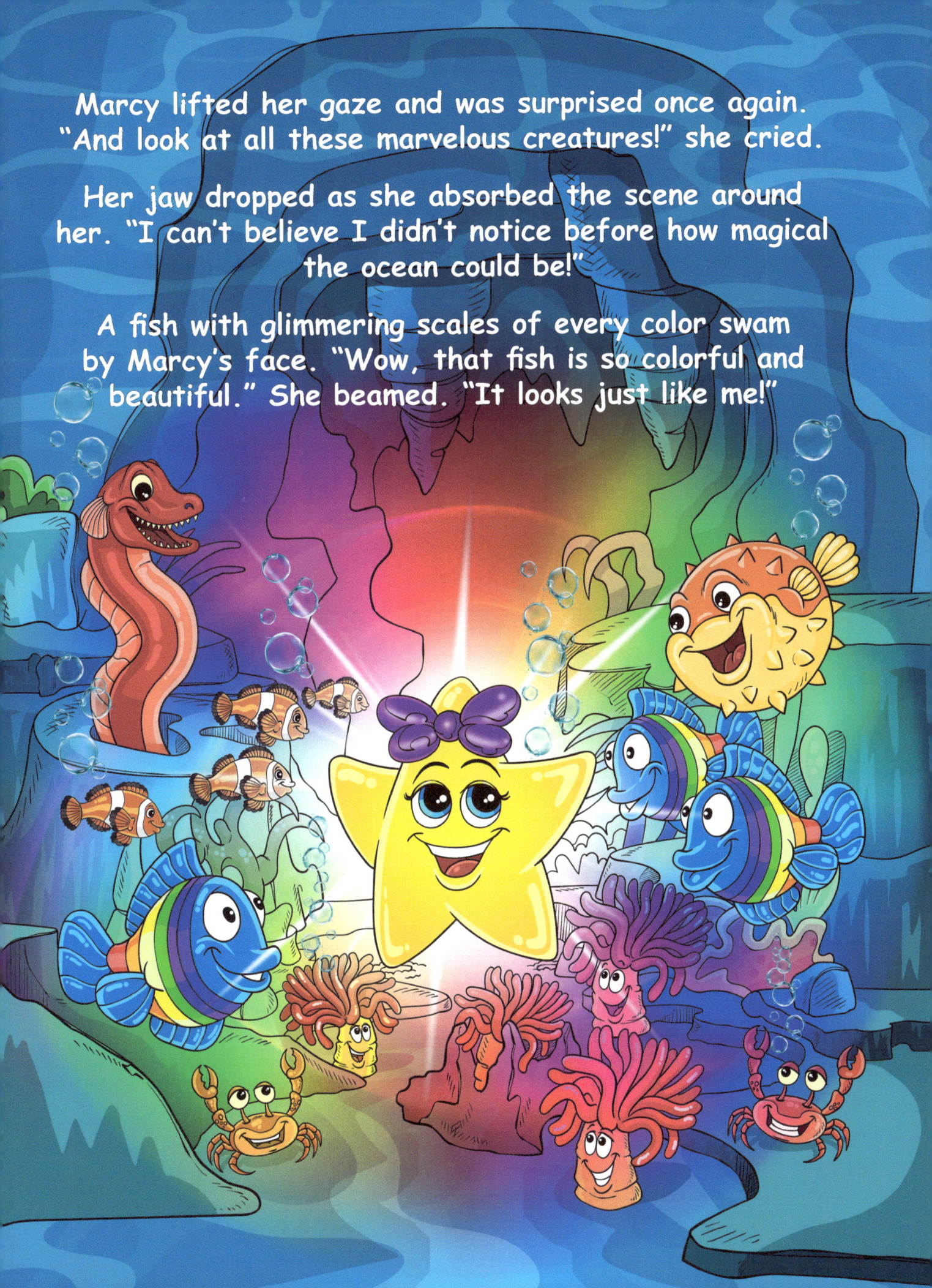

Marcy lifted her gaze and was surprised once again. "And look at all these marvelous creatures!" she cried.

Her jaw dropped as she absorbed the scene around her. "I can't believe I didn't notice before how magical the ocean could be!"

A fish with glimmering scales of every color swam by Marcy's face. "Wow, that fish is so colorful and beautiful." She beamed. "It looks just like me!"

Suddenly, the sand below her began to rumble and fear flashed over Marcy again. A strange creature that looked like the rings of Saturn emerged from the sand.

"Who are you, and what are you doing here?!" Marcy shrieked.

"Don't be afraid, dear. I am a stingray, and I am here to help you!" The stingray gently shook the rest of the sand off his back and looked at Marcy.

"My friend the shark told me you're trying to get back to the sky, and I know someone who can help."

"Oh I can't believe it!" Marcy clapped her hands and a smile stretched across her face. "Finally, someone who can help me!"

"Come on, then!" The stingray tilted his chin up toward his back. "Hop on my back and I can take you there!"

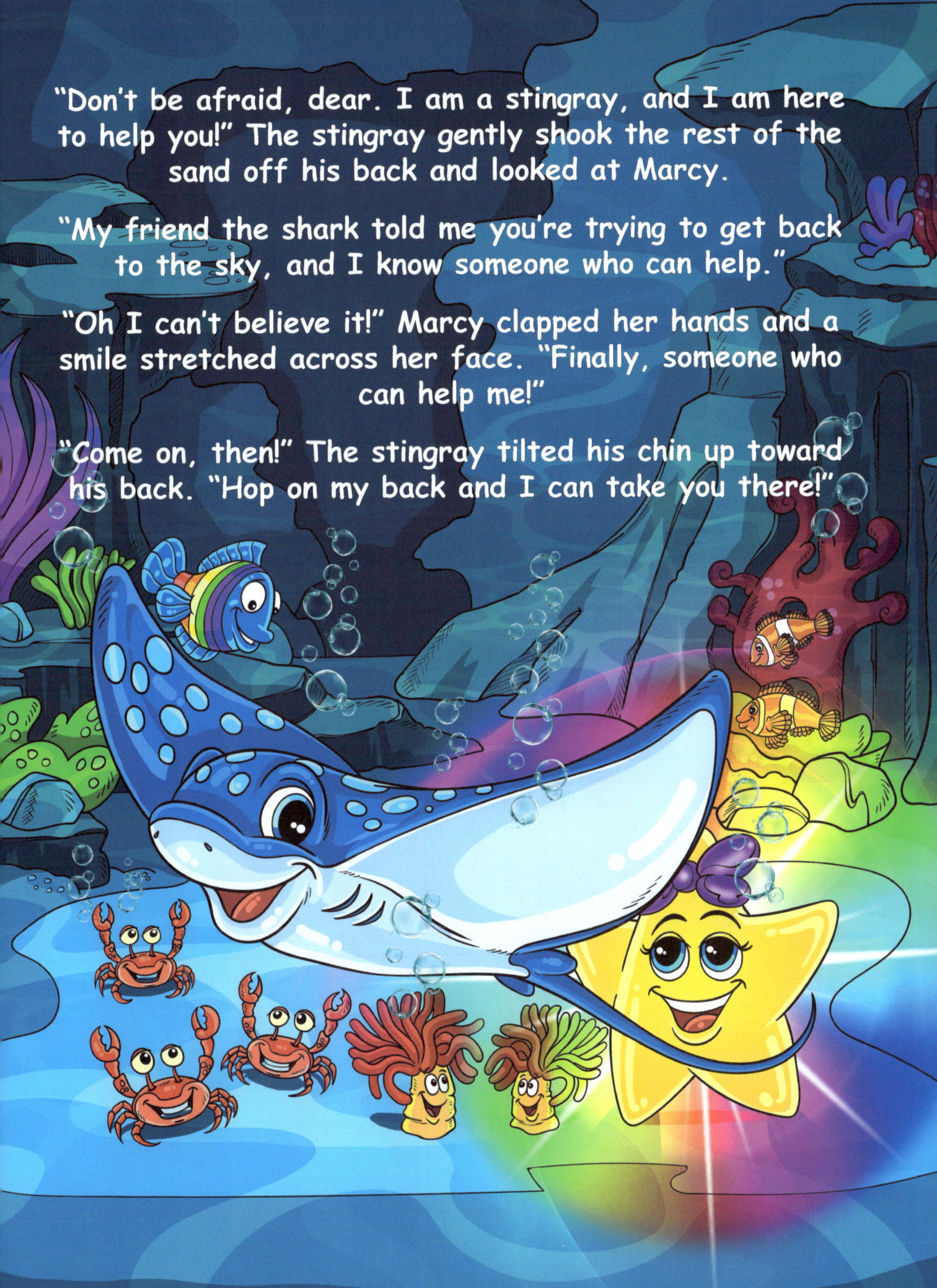

Marcy's eyes twinkled as she perched on the stingray's slick yet sturdy back.

As they glided through the ocean waves, Marcy felt a rush come over her. She saw all kinds of magical ocean creatures soar past her like a dazzling meteor shower.

Finally, the stingray and Marcy approached a giant blue figure as big as a spaceship and as still as the starry night.

"Hi, Blue. This is my friend, Marcy. She's lost here in the ocean and hopes you can help her get back to the sky," the stingray said.

"Hi, Marcy, I'm Mr. Blue Whale. Good to meet you." The majestic mammal smiled down at Marcy. "Oh, what a marvelous glow you have, my dear! You look like a glorious rainbow!"

"Thanks, Mr. Blue," Marcy said. "I didn't always like my glow, but my new ocean friends taught me that it's okay to be different. Now, I'm not as afraid to stand out."

"It sounds like your time in the ocean hasn't been so bad, then," said Mr. Blue. "But if you are ready to go home, climb onto my back and wait over the blowhole on the top of my head."

Marcy turned to face Mr. Blue and the stingray. "Thank you both so much for being kind to me and helping me find my way," she said. "And, please, thank Mr. Shark, too!"

Marcy scurried atop the giant whale. She took a deep breath, puffed out her chest and said, "I'm ready!"

Mr. Blue nodded and became very still. "Alright then, on the count of three!"

Marcy felt Mr. Blue's giant body rumble and shake. She shut her eyes tight as Mr. Blue counted down.

"One...two...three..."

"HOOOOMMMEEE!!!!"

Marcy blinked—and was surprised to find she was already back in the sky. She spotted a cluster of shiny objects nearby.

"Is that a school of fish?" Marcy squinted and then realized it was Roger and the stargang!

"Yo, look! It's our girl Marcy." Roger tossed his hair and strutted toward her. "Look who finally decided to come home."

Roger paused, peered over his glasses, and narrowed his gaze. "Oh—and she got a new glow! Where have you been, Marcy? And what's up with your colors?"

"It doesn't matter where I've been, Roger." Marcy stood up tall and looked him straight in the eye. "But what does matter is I finally learned that I can only be who I am, no matter what color—or colors—I shine!"

"So what?" Roger glared at her and turned up his nose. "Just because you have shimmering colors doesn't mean you can shine as bright as us."

Marcy paused and reflected on all the wonderful creatures she met on her journey, herself included.

After a moment, she turned to face the group. "Here, let me show you! One...two...three..."

"GLLOOWWW!"

With a burst of light, Marcy's radiant rainbow glow lit up the entire galaxy. Roger and the stargang's jaws dropped and they gazed wide-eyed at Marcy in awe.

"Wow, that was kinda cool!" Roger smiled and walked toward Marcy. "I'm sorry I made fun of your glow, Marcy. I guess your colors are what make you...well, YOU!"

"Yeah! Maybe we should try shining different colors, too!" the stargang cheered in the background.

Reassured by their reaction, Marcy turned and flashed a playful smirk toward the stars. "Well, then, show me what you got!"

Roger gleamed and motioned to the stargang. "Come on, everyone, you heard her!" he called. "Let the colors flow! And let's put on a great show tonight!"

Then, Marcy, Roger, and the whole stargang took off like lightning, shooting brilliant sparks of red, orange, blue, green, and every shade in between all over the glowing night sky.

THE END

Mallory Thayer originally wrote *Marcy Finds Her Glow* as a pre-teen, and after nearly two decades, she is finally sharing it with the world. "We are all just like Marcy," she says. "We all need to learn to overcome insecurities and accept what makes us unique, what makes us different." One of the key lines from this book  is a real-life mantra Mallory and her mother, Janice, have been saying to each other as encouragement for years: "I can only be who I am." She hopes that children and parents alike are inspired by this mantra and story about accepting your true colors.

Mallory grew up and lived most of her life in the Midwest, spending much of her childhood writing imaginative stories. She received a Bachelor's degree from Indiana University and a Master's in Public Administration from The Ohio State University. Mallory is an aunt to three lovely nieces and is a committed cat mom. She loves to travel, and her favorite destination is the Czech Republic—she even speaks Czech! In addition to being an author and world traveler, Mallory is a yoga enthusiast, avid puzzler, disco music aficionado, and groovy bass player. She lives in Atlanta, GA. This is her first book. To learn more, **follow her on Instagram (@mallory_writes_xoxo) or visit mallory-writes.com.**

Jeanine Henning started illustrating at 3 years old (with her mom's red Revlon on the newly painted white wall). 25 Years in the media industry later, she is still passionate about bringing authors' imaginations to life. Jeanine is a Moonbeam Children's Book Award Gold winner, among a tally of other awards. When not illustrating, she's out hiking or spending time with her dog. To see more of Jeanine's work, visit jeaninehenning.com.

www.ingramcontent.com/pod-product-compliance
Lightning Source LLC
Chambersburg PA
CBHW041411010526
44107CB00015B/1134